My Book of Poems

Depression, Obsession

Deborah Anne Kimberley

Owner and author Deborah Anne Kimberley- 403 830 Esquimalt Road Victoria
British Columbia September 14th, 2008
Copyright registration no 484261
Date of registration: April. 25th 2000
No: 98/2184
I SAY THAT IF A DECISION IS NOT MADE UNDER THE PROVISIONS
SET OUT IN THE
AFFIDAVIT THREE AND IN THIS AFFIDAVIT ONE Dated January 30th,
2015, I say that the British
Government The United States Government should go after the Canadian
Government for the
compensation/relief that I refer to in Affidavit three and the Affidavit of Dr.
Linda and this affidavit and in MY Will and my Statement of Claim that I do
and will swear that this information and all other information before the courts
now or in the future is true and correct and to the best of my knowledge.

Dedication

I dedicate my book of poems, *Depression Obsession,* to all the babies, children, and all the people in the world who suffer from Crohn's disease, and of course, to my representation.

Table of Contents

Page Blank Intentionally

Preface

I slowly started writing "My Book Of Poems" and "Depression Obsession" around 1993 after I had admitted myself to Eric Martin Institute, which is part of the Jubilee Hospital in Victoria, British Columbia, Canada. I also worked there. "My Book Of Poems" started out to be the trashy explanation about the cycle of abuse that didn't really apply to me. I have been documenting the stalking, harassment, and mental abuse since 1982, some of which was stolen from me, and it is still ongoing. That inspired me to write my three books. It took me until just recently to figure this all out with the help of my representative. However, I didn't have any apparent help writing "My Book of Poems."

I found myself being forced to go to Eric Martin for thirteen years just because I was sure there was something physically wrong with me. I was always reassured by all the many so-called professionals I saw that there was nothing physically wrong, but I couldn't let it go; I was so ill. Even after requesting my medical files, all I received was a bunch of nonspecific diagnoses of my so-called mental health. Years later, I started to do some research in the library at Eric Martin and realized that I had Post Traumatic Stress Disorder from all the trauma I experienced in my life. (60 years of it now, totally premeditated.) But there was much more to my illness and deep down I knew that.

After I was secretly treated for bladder carcinoma, I found a copy of a report in my living room one day, indicating I had Pelvic Inflammatory Disease, which I was born with. Through my father's past history, I was able to figure out that Pelvic Inflammatory Disease was a form of Crohn's Disease, which my representative informed me is curable. I just recently decided to have my books published so everyone inflicted with this God-awful disease and abuse, which no one should have to go through, could hopefully do something about it.

Death Came Knocking at My Door.

I Took a Trip Down Insanity Lane,
I Know This Kind of Pain.
I'm Not Afraid to Die Anymore,
As Death Came Knocking at My Door.

A Little Girl Pulled a Trigger Inside,
And Blew Up the Feelings
The Evil Government's Underground Worlds
Taught Me to Hide.
They Are All Crazy and Greedy as Assessed,
And Their Evil They Had Me Suppress.

It Is Not Impossible to Have No Recall.
Of Childhood, The Mobs All Robbed.
They Wanted Me Dead
So, I Would Not Tell,
This I Know All Too Well.

I pray to God for The Evil Governments
And Their Underground Worlds,
As The Lord Is with Me in Their Turmoil.
He Stands Beside Them and Tries to Help Them Along,
With Our Father Is Where We All Belong.

So, I took a Trip Down Insanity Lane,
To Help Take Our Dignity Back Again,
And We Want You To Know We Can't Take Anymore.
As Death Is Now Knocking at All of Our Doors.

Deborah Anne Kimberley

Depression Obsession

Locked In a Prison Cell
In The Beginning of Time
Spirits They Are in Composition
Crying All of The Time
Pacing And Not Knowing Why
Traumatized My Heart Pounding Immense
Physical And Emotional Pain
Like A Migraine All Over My Body
And The Evil Say It's Growing Pains
Suffocation, so I can't breathe
My Throat Is Closing Up
I Can't Swallow, I Gag
Uncontrollable Shaking
Ears Ringing with Insanity
The Evil
Continually Running Free
In Hunt to Kill Off Humanity
I'm Still Dying
Because of The Evil Government's Underground Worlds

Spirits They Are in Composition
I Became a Child of God Once Again.

The Wolf That Cries

Target Of Violence
They Are Ferocious Animals
The Panic the Stillness
No Release or Relief
The Wolf That Cries
Through Whispering Pines
Is Their Sly Fox
Their Glimmer Their Thrust
Hunted Prey
The Wolf That Cries
Their Sounds in The Wilderness
They Are Delusional Bears
In The Mutilation
The Swipe of Life
The Wolf That Cries

Deborah Anne Kimberley

To The World's Lost Children

Dark Clouds of Terror,
Worldwide in Confusion,
They Strike with Their Lightning Bolts,
Participants Paralyzed by Their Delusions.
Split Second Quakes,
Are There Cracks in Foundations?
Another Dimension,
No Realization.
Heights of Their Hurricanes,
Rampaging Wild,
Trapped in a Funnel,
Unravelling A Child.
To The World's Lost Children
It's Devastation at Its Worst,
Violation and Crime,
Launched Into Life Cursed,
And You Have All Spent the Time,

The Evil Governments and Their Underground Worlds Who Are Evil, Greedy, And One of a Kind.

A Spirit Composition Arose.
Outrageously Out of Their Body,
Outrageously Out of Their Minds.
Your Steel-Clad Doors Were Locked Closed.
When A Spirit Composition Arose
Volcano Eruptions Fester Within
Fiery Inferno Bubbling Sins.
Scrambling for a Place to Hide,
Outrageously Out of Their Body,
Outrageously Out of Their Minds.
Knives They Pierce in Blood So Thick,
Pouring Lava Is Beginning to Stick,
Fleeting Powers Don't Subside,
Outrageously Out of Their Body,
Outrageously Out of Their Minds.

I Still Wake to Catch My Breath
In Darkness
The Spirit Composition Left.

Deborah Anne Kimberley

In My Wildest of Dreams

In The Midst of a Lake,
Going Under: Life Is at Stake.
Too Far Out They Did Swim,
There Is No Hope for Any of Them.

In The Midst of a Quake,
We're Going Down for God's Sake,

On Top of the Eleventh Floor,
Plastered Against the Sliding Glass Doors.
The Building Collapsed
On Top of Me.

The Evil Government's
Underground World
Were My Wildest Dreams.
With Open Eyes They Will Never See,
Their Extremely Deleterious Insanity.

Life In Their Hell

The Nightmares So Deep,
A Child Afraid to Go to Sleep,
So Many Lives in One Heap,
All Their Souls They Will Keep.

These Demons Create Trouble in School,
Their Dirt and Names Are Their Tools,
They Are Nothing but Evil, Greedy Fools.

They Love Their Playground,
For Their Anger That Calls.
Drug Addicts as They Crawl,
Inside Their Insane Walls.

Can't Stand Them and Dwell,
From Their Pain I Know Well.
And I Am So Afraid to Tell,
Every Time That They Fell Of
Life In Their Hell.

Deborah Anne Kimberley

The Whole World Is Sleeping

The Whole World Is Sleeping,
The Walls Caving In.
I am in A Small Box,
Where Isolation Begins.

The Whole World Is Sleeping,
As I Try to Get Out.
But The Box It Gets Smaller,
And My Heart Stops and Starts.

The Whole World Is Sleeping,
I Can't Wake It Up.
This Box Is so soundproof,
And I'm Made of Soft Stuff.

The Whole World Was Sleeping,
When I Ran Out of Air.
And entered an Unbelievable Nightmare,
So, We Could All Be Spared.

The Whole World Is Sleeping,
I Can't Wake It Up.

My Own Little World

My Arms Were Aching,
And when I reached them out,
I Found That There Were Children About.
I Looked Through Those Innocent Eyes,
Wind Behind Me and the Sun on My Face
Life's Painted Picture Came Alive
As My Heart That Bleeds Begins to Race.

Suddenly I'm High on A Swing
Above The Clouds
Doing Child-Like Things.
I jumped to The Ground
And Begin to Twirl
I'm Off in My Own Little World.

Hopping, Skipping, Running Through
Life's Forsaken Garden's Gate,
Holding Wonders I Wished I Knew.
Vivid Roses, Red and Sweet
Teardrops Glistening
On Velvet Pedals Meet.

Then I Got This Sweeping Urge
To Take the Socks Off My Feet
And Chase the Birds.
Flapping Echoes of Wings in Their Flight
The Sky Opens Up
They Fly into the Drakes of The Night.

Now I Am Standing in Those Innocent Eyes.
The Wind in Front Of me is Blowing Dark Clouds in the Skies.
My Life's Painted Picture Long Ago Died.
And My Heart That Bleeds Now Knows Why I Cry.

Deborah Anne Kimberley

Quite Little Footsteps

Quite
Little Footsteps
You Can't See Me
But I Am Real
Quite
Little Footsteps
You Can't Touch Me
Cause I Can't Feel
Quite
Little Footsteps
You Can't Hear Me
As I'm Not Heard
Quiet
Little Footsteps
Now In Solitude
And I Observe
That
Quite
Little Footsteps
Are Inside Myself
And I'm Not Alone
And My
Quite
Little Footsteps
Will Never Be Known

Promised Land

In The Winter's Candle Light,
Angels Touch the Soles in Flight.
A Gentle Breeze Brushed Over Me,
The Promised Land Has Set Me Free.

In Wonder Land Without a Shield,
Bright Eyed and Emerald Fields.
Seas of Flowers Soft and Pure,
The Air You Breathe Provides a Cure.

Life Thereafter Sustains No Fear,
The Winding Rivers Are Crystal Clear.
There Is No Such Darkness Far Above,
And There We Learn the Gift of Love.

So, in the Winter's Candlelight,
Angels Touched My Soul That Night.
The Gentle Breeze That Brushed Over Me,
Was The Promised Land That Will Set Some Free?

Deborah Anne Kimberley

The Silence Is Breaking

In The Echoes of All Sane Minds.
True Love Is Very Hard to Find.
The Silence Is Breaking
Over Time.
It is Horribly Painful,
It Is Unbelievably Unkind.

My Nightmares, They Will Never Go.
Fear, Grief, And Anger
I Have Known.

The Silence Is Braking
Over Time.
I Am a Survivor.
The Wind It Won't Go.
You Can Not Mend,
What You Can Not Sew.

The Silence Is Braking
Over Time.
In Life's Rugged, Rocky Land.
Forever Holding Hands.
As I make a Firm, Strong Stand,
The Silence Is Braking
For All of Man.

I Ran with The Wind

I Need to Be Held Tight,
I want to Know If It Will be all Alright,
I'm A Caring Person,
I Know What Love Is.

God Has Given Me A Message to Send.
Of the Cruelty in Men,
Who was born with A curse,
There Couldn't Be Anything Worse.

To Become Full of Fear,
I Honestly Speak with Flooding Tears.
God Was with Me in My Pain,
When I Said

God, Please Let Me Do Good someway
A Child of God
That Believes That He Did
Because Suddenly I Ran with The Wind.

Deborah Anne Kimberley

My Lord's Prayer

Now I Lay Me Down to Sleep,
I pray the Lord, My Soul to keep,
And if I Die Before I wake,
I Pray the Lord My Soul to Take.

God Bless Mom and Dad
My sister and Brothers
Their Husbands and Wives
My Aunts and Uncles
My Cousins and Their Children
Grandmothers And Grandfathers
My Children
My Nieces and Nephews
And All the Babies, Children, And People of the World.

Dear Lord,
Please Make Me Do Good Someway.
I Promise I Won't Ask for Anything Else
Because
I Don't Want to Be Greedy.
I Know There Are Lots Of
Babies, Children, And People
All Suffering in the World
Who Aren't as Lucky As I

So, I Pray That I Have Done Good Someway.

Remember The United Nations

Remember The United Nations, So Much They Are Worth.
They Face the Turmoil of This Earth.
Put On Their Shoes and Crawl Underground.
In The Underground Maze Were The
Underground Blackness Surrounds.

They Have Lights So They Can See.
All The Destruction in The
Underground World Which Runs Free.
They Can Not Afford to Be Afraid.
For Beneath an Underground World
Humanity Will Then Stay.

The United Nations Knows the Direction to Take.
As They Have Seen
The Death of Innocent Lives and Those at Stake.

Believe in All These Underground Worlds
There Is a Judgment Day.
When Their Victims No Longer Have to Pay.

The United Nations, They're A Computer Whiz.
What These Underground Worlds Feed Humanity
We, As Real People, Can Not Let Live.

So, The United Nations' Information Gets Filed Away.
To Be Reprogrammed Again Someday.
To Put the Underground World at Bay.
Know That the Good in Humanity Never Runs Astray.

Remember The United Nations, So Much They Are Worth.
They Face the Turmoil on This Earth.

Thank you For All the Times the United Nations has saved My Life.

Deborah Anne Kimberley

No Man's Land

We Trudge Along This Twisted Road.
Their Road of Dirt Man Will Not Stand.
We Carry Such a Heavy Load.
With A Map Of
No Man's Land.

In No Man's Land.
No One Ever Grows.
Only Insanity Flows.
And The Hawks Are Flying Low.

All Their Garbage Spews About.
In A Bug Infested Pit.
And Here We Throw Our Rubbish Out.
There Is No Way to Salvage It.
In No Man's Land.

So, We Trudged Along This Twisted Road.
Their Road of Dirt Man Will Not Stand.
Still Carrying Such a Heavy Load.
And A Map Of
No Man's Land.

As In No Man's Land
There Is No Respect For
Humanity.

My Mother's Loves

The Demons Had My Mother's First Husband Crushed with Logs.
A Three-Week-Old Baby Little Welfare to Live On.
Forced Back to Her Folks Who Ran Board and Room.
A Farm on Acreage That They Tried to Run Too.

She Cooked and She Cleaned and She Tried to Be Mom,
The Demons and Their Underground World Said Poison Her Son.
Come to Grandpa, the Crazy Old Man Would Say,
The Boy for Good Reason Continually Ran Away.

My Brother Was Six When Mom married an Army Man,
And The Demons Took All His Cash Right Out of the Palms of His Hands.
But Some Insurance Money from Mom's First Husband's Death,
Bought Them the Things That They Needed with Nothing Else Left.

Well, The Evil Demons Born Babies, Bloody Well Cursed.
And In Canada, I Just Happened to Be the Unfortunate First.
So, at the Age of one,
Mom Took Us by Train to Where All the Demons ' Battles begun.

Dad Became Allergic to Wool, You See.
So, We Couldn't Be Posted Overseas.
A Pretty Piss Poor Excuse,
For All the Evil Demons
Insanity, Filth, And Greed.

So, We Lived in a Real Nightmare,
Looking Back at My Life, There Has Got to Be Heaven Somewhere.

Now, Decades Later, Around the World, There's the Start of a War,
The Silence Has Broken Afar.

Who'd Believe the Way That I Figured Out,
What The Hell was this all About?
How All the Evil Demons and Their Underground World Came to Slaughter,
A Loving Man and His Loving Daughter.

My Dad to Me Will Always Be the Best Man in the Whole Wide World
Who I Love with All My Heart and Soul.

A Vet of Two World Wars Who Fought Against the Evil Insane Governments

Deborah Anne Kimberley

from All Around
The World Purposely Made Suffer a Slow, Miserable, Agonizing Death, And
Then He Was Laughed at His Death Bed, And as Sick as That All Is, These
Outrageously Insane and Piss Poor Excuses for Human Beings Really
Enjoyed Every Minute of It.

Crohn's Disease, Which Has Been Discovered to Be This So-Called Genetic
Composition. However, It Is All the Evil Government's Support for The Roman
Catholic Religion and The Likes of all Their Sexually Transmitted
Diseases Which They Continually Inflict on Innocent Men, Women, and
Children
And Helpless Newborn Babies and Have Done So for Centuries and Still
Counting All for the Evil Governments and Their Underground
Insanity, Filth, And Greed.

My Dad Worked the Fields at a Very Young Age, Cause at Three all the Evil
Governments
And Their Underground Worlds Had His Protestant Father Snuffed Away.
Dad Worked His Fingers to The Bone, And His Roman Catholic Mother
Remarried, So She
Could Sit on A Throne.

Well, To Do That, She Continually Had a Whole slew of Kids
Forced My Dad to the Army Hoping He Too Would Get Done In.
When That Didn't Work, They Married Him Off to a Slut
Now There Is Hell to Pay Cause Health Care in Canada Is in a Huge Rut.

Dad's Dirty Wife She Went and Gave Birth
And Dad Got Them Both, But He Just Kept the First.
So, His Insane Mother Looked After Dad's Boy
As In the Evil Army, Dad Was Employed.

They Then Posted Him So He Could Meet My Mom
And That Is How This God-Awful Story Begun.

Two Wars Later, After Picking Up the Dead
He Turned to Booze to Drown Memories Raging in His Head.
But He Faithfully Paid for His Two Kids
Making A New Life for the Better of Him.

Dad, He Would Be Away Drinking to Try and Make Amends
Paying For It by Helping Outrageously Insane Men.
Those Evil Beings Are All to Blame

My Book of Poems: Depression, Obsession

Once, My Poor Dad Caught the Couch Aflame.
Well, He Left the Evil Army because he was afraid
They Kicked His Ass Out the Door with No Trade.
Dad's Drinking It Slowed Right Down
But All These Evil Demons Kept Sniffing Around.

Dad Felt Guilty for Leaving His Son
And Moving to Where My Mother Wanted to Belong.
So, He Eventually Bought Property for His Back
And I Bet the Evil Governments and Their Underground World
Even Took That.

So, We Rented a House on Evil Street
Remembering School There with No Defeat.
I Fell Off My Bike and Needed a Crown
Cause Of That Crazy Old Gramps Who the Evil Governments and Their
Underground World Told to Run Her Right Down.

Dad And My Brother built us a New Home
And Mom and Dad Felt So Lucky to Have a Small Loan.
The Evil Demon Had Poisoned That Kid
So That Is Why My Brother Acted the Way He Did.

The Evil Demons and Their Underground World
Forced Me as a Child to Learn,
Putting Innocent Children Up to It for A Turn
And My Brother, They Made Him Pay
But Now the Real Demons Are All About to Get Laid.

Well, We Moved into Dad's House at Christmas Time
And For Our Family, Nothing Has Ever Been Fine.
Even Though My Brother Graduated
All Of Our Lives:
The Evil Demons and Their Underground World
Big Time Terminated.
My Dad Only Had Grade Four, So My Brother Got Busy
And Taught Him Some More,
And I Repeated This Grade
And My Mother Said Grade Ten Is All I Made.

So, I Toughed It Out on My Own
And I'd Cry at Nights All Alone,
The Catholics Ran Kids Over with Bikes

Deborah Anne Kimberley

And Then They'd All Try to Pick Fights.
The Evil Governments and Their Underground Worlds
Bribe Small Children to Sexually Molest,
And They Add Terrorist Acts to The Insanity of All This.

My Cousin and I Would Get in the Demon Gramps' Car
He'd Scare the Shit Out of Us the Roman Catholic
Would Take It Way Too Far,
One Time the Back Door He Didn't Shut and I Was Getting Sucked Right Out.

That Sick Catholic Prick Would Laugh So Damn Hard
When He Did This, He Wouldn't Stop the Car.
He Was Served Well All of His Life
As It Was Decided, He Was to Get His Jollies with Fright.

A Metal End of a Blower to Get Caught in My Throat No Lower and Six Hours
Of It Cutting My Throat in Their Spite till The Family Hero Dr. Turd Decided
To Save My Life.

Dad Got Sick When I Was Ten
And My Brother Was Seventeen and A Half Then,
All The Sick, Evil Quacks Said That They Checked Him Right Out, But Kid,
You
Not These Sickos Knew Exactly What All the Pain Was About.

You Shouldn't Drink No More, They Said
But They Still Got Together to Close His Door Instead.
So, When Dad Quite Drinking, The Torture Began, And
It Makes Me Sick What They Did To That Poor Man.

By Mid Teens
The Evil Demons and Their Underground Worlds Got Out of Hand,
There Was No Way to Stick Up for Myself Cause the Evil Governments And
Their Underground Worlds Made Sure That My Mouth Was Kept Shut With
Their Trauma, Deceit, Street Drugs, And Their Smut.

And So, All the Evil Governments and Their Underground Worlds
Did This and So Much More,
And It Starts with The Greed in Their Insanity
Doubled With the Disrespect for All of Humanity.

My Poor Cousin

My Poor Cousin, A Sick Auntie's Daughter,
Didn't Give a Dam How the Evil Demons' Underground World
Have The Likes of Her Slaughtered.

A Mind of an Eight-Year-Old Is What They Said,
Gave Her Medication to Kick Her Off Dead.
Well, All the Evil Demons Who Help Terrorize Helpless Little Kids
Who are From
Hell Is Crazy Now, Hay, Evil Demons in Your Underground Worlds.

Well, My Sick Auntie Never Made Any Time to See What Really Went On
In An Epileptic's, My Poor Cousin's Mind.
She Let the Evil Demons' Underground World Care for Her
So, They All Could Go About Their Work.

On My Sixteenth Birthday, My Mother Told Me Your Cousin Is Dead.
Died Of a Brain Clot Is What Those Sick Demons Said.

I Know the Lord Is Looking After Her for Sure.
My Cousin You Were Never Heard.

I Have Missed You. I Want to Thank You for Saving My Life. I Hope This
Will
Do. God Rest Your Sole.

Deborah Anne Kimberley

My Mother's Two Sinister Sisters

Mom's Two Sinister Sisters Married Navy Guys,
The Federal Service Has Cheap Alcohol for Their Disguise.
But That Wasn't Good Enough for Any of Them, You See, So the Evil Demons
Underground World Sucked the Living Life Out of My Dad in All Their
Filth And Greed.

All That Cash for Their Payment That They All Must Have Made,
For Decades, They Have Gotten Away with This Vindictive Brigade.
At The Screwed-Up Family Gatherings They'd Treat My Family Like Shit,
But Out of Respect, We Put Up with It.

They Would Taunt Us with How's Your Guts?
The Demons Knew Just What the Pain Was All About.
We had the Same Quack whose Fee Was Prolonging Agony for All Their Filth
And Greed.

For The Likes of Them, It Was a Real Thriller to Inflict This Suffering Without
A Damn PainKiller.
For These Evil Demons, Big Dollar Signs They Did See,
And No One Ever Thought Twice of Being So God Forsakenly Mean.

So, My Sinister Auntie's Police Son Was Promoted to the RCMP Detachment
For All His Fun,
These Evil demons and their drugged-up underground Operations
Thought Was Well Done.

All These Evil Demons and Their Drugged Underground Operations Put
Me Through the Same Kind of Crap,
But They Are Not Getting Away With it, because
Yes, Sirs, All You Shrinks and Quacks
I Like to Hear Myself Yap.

To Wrap Up This Story, Look at Our Health Care Now, One Hell of a Mess.
I Don't Know About You, But All This Is Hard to Digest.

Crooked Uncle Max

Over I Went with My Suitcase Packed,
To Baby Sit for The Crooked Uncle Max.
Who Climbed Right to the Top, What A Man,
When He Deserved to Sleep in A Garbage Can.

He Never Finished at the Roman Catholic School,
So, This Was His Part With
All The Evil Demons and The Underground World's Approval.

He had a Home on A Platter, driving a Company's Car,
And He Once Took the Family to Dinner on His Business Master Card.
But Mom and Dad, They Paid Him with Cash And
He Pocketed It as If They Were Trash.

Once He Gave Me A Telephone to take with Me When I Went Home,
My Mother Despised Him for Doing All This, And That Is When She Stopped
My Visits.

Well, When His Parents Died, He Ran His Lying Ass Right Over,
Scooped What He Thought He Deserved
Without Paying the Bills That He Owed.
Mother's Sick and Greedy Siblings Then Took the High Road Out,
Now Everyone Is Going to Know
Just What You Lot Are About.

Deborah Anne Kimberley

The Goldfish in Grandma's Pond

The Goldfish in Grandma's Pond,
Outside The Decrypted House That's Still Not Gone.
And In Her Field of Vegetables and Plants,
Stands Some Man's Complex.

Many Pickling Jars and Jams on Her Shelves,
In a run-down pantry at the Back of Her Old House.
Worldly Aromas and Breads,
Always Lingered throughout the Air.

A Rag and an Apron Was Her Friend,
She Never Had Any Time to Spend,
But Pennies She'd Give Me and Send,
Me To the Goldfish in Grandma's Pond.

Go Make a Wish, She Would Say,
Will You Feed the Fish for Me Today?
A Cookie in Hand, I'd Run and Play With
The Goldfish in Grandma's Pond.

Well, My Dad, Who Was of English descent,
Built Them a House for Free for Mom's So-Called Payment.
And That Old Crazy Man Picked A Few Doors Down So He Could Join in
While
The Evil Demon's Underground World All Screwed Us Around.

My Scared Grandmother in Her Homemade Frocks,
And The Very First Furniture That She Ever Bought,
Wouldn't Let Her Crazy Old Man
By Her Dying Bed to Take Her Hand.

It Broke My Heart When My Grandma Died,
Just As a Mirror Image of Her Had Arrived.
At Her Dying Bed, I Took Her Hand And
She Expressed Bitterness Towards My Insane Man.

The Goldfish in Grandma's Pond
That I Never Even Wished Upon
Now's A Story of the Evil Government's Underground World's Sexual Abuse
With Their Outrageous Insanity All Running Loose.
To Which There Is Absolutely

No Excuse!

Deborah Anne Kimberley

The Evil Government at Work

When I Left This Guy a Sexual Con,
A Dude with No Last Name Who Called Himself Wrong,
Stepped In with Some Dope to Blow Up My Mind,
And His Friend Once Gave Me Velum For a Ride.

Ever since I Was Nine, Traumatic Events Raged Through My Mind,

An Axe in My Driver's Door Boy That Had Me Floored,
In A Ditch at A Mill, I Found My Toyota,
With A Blown-Up Engine, Tires Off and Rolled Over,
And If That Wasn't Enough, I Was Set Up with Dope
And I Protected All These Evil Demons So Their Drug Addicted Underground
Gangs Wouldn't Get at My Throat.

The Evil Government Wanted My Immediate Family and Me Dead.
That Was the Plan When the Evil Demons Sent Over an Englishman.
That I Felt Forced to Wed or I'd Be Eight Feet Under,
No Wonder When My Boy Was Born There Was Lightning and Thunder.

My Dad Was So Sick in All of This Turmoil,
As Now This Story Is About to Unfurl.

This Limey Was the Management of an Underground World,
A Set Up to Give Me Another One of Their Sexually Transmitted Diseases
That Kills!
So, A Year Later, when I Came Back Home After Ten Years,
My Dad Had Part of His Guts Ripped Out, Stapled, and Then Sewn.

All These Evil Demons, What the Hell Were You Thinking
A Man Who Fought for Your Freedom, And You Did This Without Even
Thinking.

Sending Our Flag Draped Over a Military Coffin.
They Said It Doesn't Happen Often.
Treating It Like a Leftover Bag.
This Was One of The Evil governments
From Around the World's Sick Underground Gags.

Well, The Evil Government and Their Underground Worlds
You Did It with Ease.
Set Ups by Roman Catholics and The Likes with Their Spread of All Their

My Book of Poems: Depression, Obsession

Sexually Transmitted Disease.
And It Has Me So Unbelievably Terrified with No Where to Turn.
Now I Send All This from Hell to the Evil Governments
Who Will Never Learn and Whose Insanity Kills.

Drug Addicted Manager.

My X Husband Was an Addicted Manager of the Underground World.
Corrupted by The Roman Catholic Religion at a Very Young Age,
And All The Addictions Of His Will Never Go Away.

He Had Insurance Money from A Motor Bike Fall,
So We Bought Land in An Underground World:
What A Bloody Bad Call.

Well, My Dad Built Us a House with one of His Friends,
Everything Done Legal to the Bitter End.
But In Eighty-Six, When the Underground World We Lived In
Got Right Out of Hand, The Underground Manager Said.

"ANYONE THAT FUCKS MY BUSINESS THAT WILL BE THE END,
IT MIGHT BE TEN YEARS FROM NOW,
BUT FOR A COUPLE OF THOUSAND DOLLARS,
NO ONE WILL EVER BE ABLE TO TELL."

This scared the Hell Right Out of Me,
As His Red Face Was Serious, I Could See.
I Once Threw Him Out, But He Came Back.
I Felt Like My Children
And I was trapped.
Well
I Prepared to Leave Him the Best That I Could.
With No One To Turn to But an Underground World
And Before I Knew it:
The Insane Drug Addicted Manager of the Evil
Government's Underground World Made Me So Physically Sick.
Then
More Insane Underground Demons Kept Adding to All of This.

The World's Mirror.

I Took a Long Look in the World's Mirror,
Things Are Not What They Once Appeared.
There's A Third World War Right Now,
As I Try to Make Dad and Others Like Him Proud.
Family To Me Means Peace for All.

Like My Dad, We Did Not Fall.
And Dad Never Did Dread,
That The Bitterness of War,
May Just Fill Our Heads.

When Dad Got Sick,
The Evil Government's Underground Worlds Dug His Grave,
But You Have to Know There Is Nothing for The United Nations' Shame.
And as a Helpless Child Who Had No Say,
So Many Others, Too,
Are Right Now Being Sleighed.

The Yes Feeling, the No Feeling
I Know the True Meaning.
It Is Something You Can Not Buy
No Matter How Much an Evil Demon Tries.
So
Take A Long Look into The World's Mirror
This Insanity Is Just What It Appears,
And the Evil Government That Won't Protect
Will Continue to Live in Fear and Their Death.

We Are All Children of God.
The Root Is All Our Trouble,
The Land of The Free Fell Among the Rubble.
Insanity Tampers with Everyone's Brain,
And Throws God's Life Right Down the Drain.

They Born Innocent Babies to suffer in Life,
That Cuts Through Sanity Like a Knife.
They Treat Them Like Damaged Goods,
And That I Have Never Understood.

Kicking Kids Right Under the Table,
You, Evil Demons, Are the Ones who are Unstable.

Deborah Anne Kimberley

You Torment Children Behind Parents' Backs,
Terrorizing Them to Make Sure That They Keep the Secrets,
Of Your Unspeakable Acts.
We Don't Want to Fear on the Day,
We Don't Want to Fear in the Night,
And Our Pain Now Is Even More of a Fright.
All The Nightmares Your Evil Demons Are Putting Us Through
And We Didn't Even Have a Clue.

You Kill Off Just to Rule, Having Thrills as A Tool.
Continually Slaughtering All God's Life
Even Though You Know What's Wrong and What's Right.
Many Others Were Not Only Hurt,
Man, They Are Eight Feet Underground Still in All Your Dirt.

We Are All Children of God,
In Whatever Way We Are Born.
You, Evil Demons, Have No Rights at All.
To Your Freedom in Any Such Form.

Don't Ever Treat Humanity That Way

I'm So Tired of All The Pain That I Am In.
And I'm Surrounded by Nothing but Sin,
My Stomach Is Turning into Knots,
Because I Am So Distraught.

It Hurts, It Hurts, It Hurts So Much,
I Tremble to Think of Anyone's Touch,
And You Don't Know Me Deep Inside,
And You Never Will Before I Die.

But I Will Somehow Save The Kids,
From All the Destruction This World Is In.
And Before I Die, I Just Want to Say
Don't You Ever Treat Me That Way.
And
Don't You Ever Treat Humanity That Way.

Deborah Anne Kimberley

Politician Ding Dongs and Political Twinkies

Violence and Crime Still Live Strong,
Because of Politician Ding Dongs.
They Allow the True Criminals to Lick Them,
So, Their Political Twinkies Can Stomp Out the Victims.

On June Twenty-Third of Nineteen-Ninety-Three,
They Must Have Introduced and Then Passed a Stocking Law Dedicated to Me.
You Can No Longer Harass or Make Yourself a Pest.
They Made It Illegal to Make Death Threats.

They Had Me Labelled Mentally Distorted When I Really Suffer From
Post-Traumatic Stress Disorder.
I Want All These Evil Demons Who Are Screwed,
To Confess to All the Tax-Paying Money They Used.
And I Want Them to Be Put Away,
Never To See the Light of Day.

Put The Politician Ding Dongs Where They Belong,
If Not, Violence and Crime Will Still Live Strong.
They Allow the True Criminals to Lick Them,
So, Their Political Twinkies Can Stomp Out the Victims.

My Book of Poems: Depression, Obsession

The Shrinks and The Quacks

The Shrinks and The Quacks Stick Tight Together,
And They Don't Give a Damn If the System They Weather.
I Have Seen So Many Quacks and So Many Shrinks, So,
Now I Can Say They Were All Evil Demons and Dinks.

The First Shrink Had a Big, Black, Bushy Moustache,
And He Kept Twirling It for His Extra Cash.
He Asked Do They Want Your Body or Your Husband's Body?

All The Shrinky Dinks They Didn't Want to Get Fucked,
As One Kept His Glasses in His Mouth for A Suck.

A Son of a Bitch Shrink Knew I Did My Homework,
And He Too Tried to Kill Me, the Murderous Jerk.

Only I Know What Goes on In My Mind.
All You Shrinks and You Quacks; I'm No Longer Blind.

Well, You Shrinks and You Quacks, I Got Your Reports
Guess, You All Thought It Was Such a Big Joke.
The Write -Ups You Make Up Are Quite the Bullshit,
You Tried Hard to Make It Look Like I Wasn't with It.

You Promoted Fucking the System Around,
Didn't Know Your Ass from A Hole in the Ground.
It is a Good Job That I Kept Track of All My Abusers,

But Now There May Be Billions of Big-time Innocent
Looser.

My Parents brought Me Up Right,
Even Though the Evil Government's Underground Was Snuffing
Out Life

So, The Shrinks and The Quacks Life You Did Rob,
Now You Are All Busted for Being Such Fuckin'
Slobs.

Deborah Anne Kimberley

Re Victimizing in This Screwed Up World.

There Are So Many People Who Love to Play God.
Who Doesn't Know What the Hell They're Doing When Life Around
The World Is Being Robbed. They Are So Institutionalized that It
It Is Hard For Them To See. So They Strut Their Stuff And Feel
So Damn Pleased.

Well, All The Evil Demons In This Government's Underground
World Will Soon Be Out Of Work, And I Am So Terrified Because
Now We Are The Dirt. There Is No Where To Run And
Nowhere to Hide And So Many Might Soon Be Doomed To Die.
If You Think That I'm Crazy, You Better Look Outside.
Now The Entire Population Will Soon Want To Die. So These Damn

Governments Better Save The Kids. That Was Why I Wanted
To Help Get Rid, What I Didn't Know The Evil Government's
Underground Worlds Did.

So All The Evil Demons From Around The World In Their High
Mucky Muck Seats Blame Yourself Not Me For This
Unbelievable Deceit. All You Evil Demons You Already
Made Me Pay. You Made Me A Pone To Try To Stop All This
Totally Outrageously And Vindictive Brigades.

Be Forever Strong If The Feeling Is Wrong.

Trust In God And The Feeling Within.
Hold Your Head High Sinners Never Win.
Let Them Know What They Say And Do Hurts.
You Must Not Let Anyone Treat You Like Dirt.

Walk Away And Don't Look Back.
Real People Do Not Attack.
As Sad As It May Seem.
Life Can Be So Ever Mean.

Within Yourself You Must Feel Proud.
Even If You Are Not With The Crowd.
Make Yourself Happy Do The Things That You Like,
As You Are Your Only Friend For Life.

Hold Your Hand Out To Guide You Along.
Be In Touch With True Love To Really Belong.
For Those Who Try And Take Advantage Of Life.
God Has Set Aside An Invisible Plight.

Seen And Not Heard Has Got To Go.
It Is A Nonsense Myth From Long Ago.
Remember Be Forever Strong.
Believe It If The Feeling Is Wrong.

In The Ocean of Peacefulness

Tranquility And Forlorned, Peace Not Yet Reached
Temporarily Found, Tossed Upon The Beach,
Decrepit Urchins, Eagle Heads, Waterlogged On Island
Beds

Seashells, Barnacles, And Tangled Slop,
Among Projecting, Polished Rocks,
Pockets Filled With Ocean Life,
To Charm Ones Wealth And Empower Delight

Mesmerizing Diamond Reflections,
The Mysterious Calm Of Misdirection.
Scavengers, Free Floating Gulls,
To Set Adrift Mormidable Dreams Upon.

In Seclusion Recognizing The Signs,
Releasing Momentary Memorability Within An
Equilibrated Mind,
No Longer To Be Subdued In A Secret Self,
For Filled With Quiet Moments Now Totally Engulfed
In The Ocean Of Peacefulness.

At The Mainstream Of My Garden's End.

At The Mainstream Of My Garden's End,
While Gathering Faith To Help Me Mend.
Unearthed With Tickling Tears Of Spring Showers,
Pure Love The Scented Breath Of An Unpicked Flower.

Emerging In The Bliss Of Natures High,
Transplanted For Creation That Once Passed Me By.
To Grow In Exploration, Astounded Simply Blown,
Along The Trails Of Discoveries Endeavouring To Know.

There Is Peace Along The Way In This Troubled World,
The Child In Me Awakes And Her Petals Do Unfurl.
A Gift Of Compassion Is Embedded To My Heart,
Of A Deep Understanding Of A Child Without A Start.

So At The Mainstream Of My Gardens's End,
While Gathering Faith To Help Me Mend
Flows A Cleansing Power One Could Pursue
In The Softly Lit Corner Of The Chosen Few.

Deborah Anne Kimberley

My Healing Heart

Within My Power Of Imagination
And The Raging War Of Indignation
I Dream The Salt Along With Ocean Waves
Could Heal My Pain And Swallow It Away.

Can You Notice The Blues In My Crystal Eyes?
The Wall Of Weeping Love In Torturous Lies
Brake Through This Torturous Weeping Love
One Will Find Purity As White As A Dove.

That Only Comes From The Unwounded Child In Me
And It Is Something You And I Will Never See
This Pain I'm Doomed To Hold Till The Day I Die
It Is Not Deserving For Anyone And I Cry,

That I Have Climbed My Highest Mountain Peeks,
And I Will Never Find Freedom, I'm So Full Of Grief.
I Know What True Love Could Have Been
But I Am Stuck With Another One's Sin.

My Healing Heart
Is Forever Understanding Of A Child Without A Start.
As I've Been Blessed With The Strength To Nurture Love.
And The Wisdom Into The Belief Of The Lord Above.

How Healed Can One Be?

How Healed Can One Be?
God Has Kept His Promise To Me
And Now I Can Really See
The Destruction In Our Society.

I Am Suffering For His Plan,
That I Can Understand
Forgiveness Holding Out My Hand
In Hopes That This Will Travel To All Of Man.

I Hope The Lord Will Promise Thee,
Life For Eternity.
And Please Forgive For All The Pain
That Might Have Been Caused In Vain.

Deborah Anne Kimberley

The Invisible Me.

A Face Of Many Masks,
I Search To Find The Key,
So I Traced Through My Past,
To Be The Invisible Me.

Look Deep Into My Eyes,
I Need To Be Freed,
Right Through The Disguise,
To The Invisible Me.

I Try To Be Strong,
As I Couldn't Let It Be,
For There Is A Part That Belongs,
To The Invisible Me.

Survival's A Task,
For Those Who Don't See,
As I Traced Through My Past,
To Be The Invisible Me.

Freedom For All

With The Closure Of Weary Eyes,
Dreaming Of Freedom
I Want To Find
In The Free Lance

The Preeminent Sculptures And Pageantry,
In This Journey Of Chance,
In The Free Lance For
Freedom That Last

The Rush Of A Natural High,
That Pulsate The Sky,
An Electrifying Stance,
Of Freedom That Lasts

The Optical Illusions And Delusions,
Theatrical Spirit In Transfusions,
Is My Poetry Enhanced,
For Freedom That Lasts

Life In Oceans Of Harmony,
Visualized To Be Our Destiny,
In The Free Lance,
Of Freedom That Lasts

Deborah Anne Kimberley

Terrorists Acts

It's Twenty-Five Years Since Writing My Life,
The Terrorists Have Caused Me So Much Fright.
Breaking Into My Homes Committing Terrorist Acts,
Taking My Medication So I'd Have A Heart Attack.

My Phone Rings Once In The Dead Of The Night,
Something That Is Not Alright,
Folded Glasses They Put On The Floor,
Breaking My Hummingbird Feeders And Much More.

Stealing My Goods Is Another One Of Their Crimes,
Toaster Oven, Microwave Set Aflame At Separate Times.
Using My Credit Card Is Another Thing,
You Never Know What Terrorist Acts They Will Bring.

Poppies Underneath My WindShield,
Looking For What They Can Steal.
Trash Beside My Name,
The Terrorists Are To Blame.

They Have The Keys To My Car,
Open My Doors, My Trunk So I Know They're Not Far.
They Have Me Stocked Wherever I Go,
With A Grin On Their Faces, However So Low.

This Kind Of Terrorist Acts,
I've Had Enough Of It That's A Fact.
This Is Only Some Of What I Know About,
The Terrorists Have Been Trying To Snuff Me Out!

It Matters a Great Deal

Thank The Time To Grow And Expand,
Thank All The Times You Held My Hand,
Thank The Time When You Begin To Feel,
Thank The Time To Know What Is Real.

Thank The Sky For It's Eternity,
Thank The Rain For It's Purity,
Thank The Sun For The Radiance,
Thank All The Flowers For Their Fragrances.

Thank The Moon In History,
Thank The Stars In Mystery,
Thank The Life A Higher College,
Thank The Inner-Self,
The Power Of Knowledge.

Thank The Time To Grow And Expand,
Thank All The Times You Held My Hand.
Thank The Time When You Pray While You Kneel,
Thank The Time
It Matters A Great Deal.

Deborah Anne Kimberley

The following poems

I dedicate to my children

I love you

I love you just the way you are
you will never be too far from my heart.

I love you
I love the things that you do
you put a smile on my face.

I love you
I love the way you look at me
those wide eyes of innocence.

I love you
I love your bubbly character
you make living out of life.

I love you
you have thoughts and feelings
just like everyone else.
that's why I say I love you
many times a day.

To my daughter

Carry Me Inside

you held my hand and it made me strong,
and when I travelled in darkness you came along,
you believed in me you did from the start,
you will always hold a very special place in my heart.

when I shed the tears of pain and remember the wrongs,
I realize that we held this indestructible bond,
and even though I was in an institution,
there's light that shines beyond all the confusion.

one can not replace this love I have for you,
I have more than enough to see me through,
you have been my saviour in life's rough ride,
and I hope that your heart will always carry me inside.

Deborah Anne Kimberley

The Anachronistic Theatre of Ignorance

In the Anachronistic Theatre of Ignorance,
The undetailed design of politics.
Where truth escapes their eyes,
Only to feed to the destruction of children's minds.

A Major Depression, unplanned to give up,
Politicians can't you see when they just had enough.
The delusive embezzlement of juggler's tricks,
Great God I've seen only illegal Pricks.

War! It's a madman's game some love to play,
And for it children so dearly pay.
But the child of a much greater God,
Is the one to suffer the juggler's odds.

Too long have children been misled,
Tormented like the living dead.
In the Anachronistic Theatre of Ignorance,
The undetailed design of politics

To my son

Born in
Thunder and lightning

Soar above the greyest of skies, only to
glide in weeping sleep rides. Shivering
and shaking,
Set me free from a tortured heart of love
aching.
Sinking among fluffy grey clouds to rest,
Ripping, tearing at thoughts suppressed.
Cursing the mental abuse some more,
Evil sins upon me like sores
A star to wish on in a night jet,
black as coal,
For an angel to cast wings on our
souls,
And capture my child, so frightened
Born in
Thunder and lightning

You will always be in my heart.

Deborah Anne Kimberley

My guest in thought AUTHOR UNKNOWN
TO ME

For my mother and father, who have passed away
Once a day, and sometimes more,
You knock upon my daydream door.
And I say warmly, "Come right in
I'm glad you're here with me again."
And we sit down and have a chat.
Recalling this and that.
Until some task that I must do
Forces me away from you-
Reluctantly, I say goodbye,
Smiling with a little sigh
For though my daydreams bring you here-
I wish that you were really here-
But what reality can't change
My dreams and wishes can be arranged-
And through my wishing, you'll be brought
To me, each day is a quest in thought.

What ever happened to

White sandy beaches
Forever reaching
The sun.

White gloves hat and purse
To sing to a verse
In church.

A white fluffy cat
That never sat
Very long.

Two beagle pups
Wanting to get up
On my lap.

The ditches filling up
Always enough
For swimming.

Us who went bowling
Not ever knowing
Who won.

The rink that dad made
Where we didn't have to pay
For fun.

A big panda bear
On the lawn chair
For me.

What ever happened to
White sandy beaches

Forever reaching
The sun.

Authors Note

I am writing this because I believe what I have to say is important. You see as a small child I was mentally abused and in my adulthood I am sill being mentally abused and for the longest time I didn't even know it was happening. I suppose at first I thought that there was something wrong with me but now I know different. I am a true survivor.

I have come to realize how necessary it is to be aware of your environment and the influences that they may have on you, that is how I have survived so far. However, this is not easy to do and when I was younger I didn't know what I could do about it so instead of going for help I ran away from it. Anyway I tried everything to try and make a friend because you see I never had a real friend and that is sad. Sometimes you think you have a friend only to realize later that this is not what you want. Mental abuse is painful but it doesn't have to be and it's not easy to try and survive on your own. It is very lonely and at times very painful.

What I learned is that the longer it goes on the more painful it becomes and running away is what causes this pain. By running away I mean drugs, alcohol, sex and even isolation.

I want to share a bit of knowledge that I never got from a book because you see I never got the opportunity to read a book. I could never concentrate. I was always thinking of three or more things at once because my world became so scary and confusing. I also skipped lines as a child.

When you are small and there has been one traumatic event after another and you don't know how to deal with it you file it away in your brain, like a computer does. In other words eventually you forget about it but it is still there. I guess you call this the subconscious. As time goes on you get so used to doing this that it becomes a habit, especially if you are told to forget about it. That is the worst thing that you can do because one day it will all come back and you may find it really hard to deal with because you never learned how before. So as the saying goes you need to find someone and tell them until they listen. Someone who doesn't have issues of their own. If you find out they do have issues of their own tell someone else, but whatever you do don't run away. Don't give up.

Another thing I learned is that it is very sad what people will do for their own benefit or maybe just to make themselves feel good and you know adults are the biggest offenders. Sometimes people inflict pain on the weak and disabled and this includes helpless children, teens and adults. This can be done without even knowing what they are really doing. Maybe what they think they are doing is for that person's own good or for the good of the community. No one and I say no one, deserves to be abused no matter what because it hurts and that person has or is suffering enough and if they think they aren't now they are only fooling themselves because it will catch up to them sooner or later. I believe it always does.

I know you have probably all heard this before but I need to tell you. Maybe I'm being selfish for once, doing something for me but I look at it too. Maybe if I help one person from going through the hell that I have it will all be worth the immense pain that I have gone through in the last twenty years of learning what my life was, really.

I have found out that if a person tries to describe your reality or is judging you that is the worst thing. Only you know what your life is like, only you know your reality. I used to think that, oh, that doesn't bother me. I'm happy, but inside of me without realizing it, I needed to help myself too and that fear can get the best of you and make your life a living hell.

To have a happy life, always think that you are just as good as the next guy and walk away if someone hurts you because real people do not attack you, they support you the best way they know how and sometimes that can be very lonely if they have problems of their own.

I wanted to give up so many times and just curl up in a little ball. But life is a miracle and that's why I'm still here.

Written for me by my representatives.

About the Author

Deborah Anne Kimberley is a survivor, truth-teller, and advocate whose life has been shaped by profound hardship, resilience, and a relentless pursuit of justice. Born in Victoria, British Columbia, Deborah's early years were marked by family upheaval, trauma, and isolation. Her journey through abuse, systemic failures, and mental health struggles led her to find a voice through writing.

Drawing from deeply personal experiences including the impacts of childhood abuse, sexual violence, institutional betrayal, and long-term harassment, Deborah's work seeks to illuminate the pain and complexity of trauma while advocating for truth and healing. She spent many years working within the Vancouver Island Health Authority and navigating the mental health system, often facing more harm than help.

Deborah's writing is raw, fearless, and rooted in lived reality. Her poetry collection, *My Book of Poems: Depression Obsession*, is both a cry for recognition and a call for change. Through her words, she invites others to look beyond stigma and listen to the stories that are too often silenced.